57 Must Use Words in Every Piece of Marketing that You Do for Your Business

John Di Lemme

57 Must Use Words in Every Piece of Marketing that You Do for Your Business

Di Lemme Development Group, Inc.
931 Village Boulevard
Suite 905-366
West Palm Beach, Florida 33409-1939
877-277-3339
www.ChampionsLiveFree.com

ISBN: 978-1-300-61378-7

About the Author

In September 2001, John Di Lemme founded Di Lemme Development Group, Inc., a company known worldwide for its role in expanding the personal development industry. As President and CEO, John strives for excellence in every area of his business and believes that you must surround yourself with a like-minded team in order to stay on top of your game.

In addition to building a successful company, John has changed lives around the globe as an international motivational speaker that has spoken in over five hundred venues. Over the past eleven years, he has shared the stage with the best of the best including Dr. John Maxwell, Rich Devos, Dennis Waitley, Jim Rohn, and Les Brown only to name a few. John has also been interviewed countless times and featured on many programs including Zig Ziglar's webcast. This is truly an amazing feat for someone that was clinically diagnosed as a stutterer at a very young age and told that he would never speak fluently.

John truly believes that everyone needs personal development to reach their full potential in life, and his determination to reach all forms of media with his motivational messages has catapulted his career. John has produced over four hundred fifty products and is an accomplished author of eleven books including his latest best-selling book, "7 Principles to Live a Champion Life." As a Strategic Business Coach, John's students include doctors, lawyers, entrepreneurs, consultants, CEOs of million dollar companies and various other occupations that are thriving in a so-called poor economy. John's success with his students has made him one of the most highly sought after business coaches in the world.

John's passion is to teach others how to live a champion life despite the label that society has placed on them. Through his books, audio/video materials, sold-out live seminars, numerous television interviews, intensive training boot camps, weekly tele-classes, Strategic Business Coaching, Closing & Marketing University, Millionaire Affirmation Academy, and Lifestyle Freedom Club memberships, John has made success a reality for thousands worldwide.

Introduction

Contained in the pages of this book are fifty-seven proven, time-tested, must use words that will explode ANY business guaranteed! When you finish reading this book you are going to say to yourself, “I just got so much information that I just legally ripped off John Di Lemme!” The highly-guarded marketing strategies that I've shared within these pages will be worth millions of dollars of income to someone's business. It's your decision whether or not it will be you!

These words are essential for anyone that develops marketing pieces for their business. It could be a flyer you’re handing out, an advertisement you're pitching, a promotion you're running, a postcard you're mailing, a one-on-one presentation you're doing, a website you are building, or anything else you are using to promote your business.

These fifty-seven words will be invaluable tools for anyone involved in sales and marketing or any type of sales. All fifty-seven may not specifically be applicable to you, but I guarantee that whether you apply one of these words or all fifty-seven to your marketing, it will skyrocket your results in business and you will earn more income!

Every mistake that I've ever made in my business was because I had no one to go to who had been there, done it, paid the price, and paid the penalty. As a part of my life's mission, I am here to be your mentor and strategic business coach and to share the tools and secrets that I have discovered to be the key to true success! I assure you that what I'm going to share with you in this book are the secrets I use on a daily basis that have brought my business record-breaking success.

Now, let's get to it! I'm going to share each of the fifty-seven words and then give you an example of how you can use it in your marketing.

57 Must Use Words in Every Piece of Marketing You Do for Your Business

Word #1: Shocking

"This is a *Shocking Offer*! You're gonna be shocked out of your mind by what I'm going to allow you to steal from me today." Use the word shocking to grab the attention of your buyer and plant the expectation in their mind that they are going to grab a hold of an amazing offer.

Word #2: Absolutely

"When you make a decision today to do business with our company, you will absolutely get the results that you desire." This word erases the doubt out of the mind of the person reading your marketing material. They will know that they can depend on you.

Word #3: Equally Crazy

"Not only do you get one of my top motivational products, but what's equally crazy is that you also get a ticket to my annual *3* Day Why Warrior Private Event. That's equally crazy!" You can use this word to throw an awesome bonus on top of your already unbelievable deal that you are marketing to your clients. This makes a really great crazy deal even crazier!

Word #4: Tremendous Value, Ridiculous Offer

"Today and today only I'm gonna allow you to invest in this absolutely shocking, ridiculous offer of tremendous value." How many of you just wanna buy something when I say that? Do you see how that works?

Word #5: Relationship Building

"My goal in my business is to build long-term relationships with my clients." Today, most business is referral driven. So, it's important for you to convey to your customers that you are looking to build a long-term relationship with them.

People want to hear that and want to know that they can trust you to be there when they need your product or services.

Word #6: Must Own

I use this one a lot in my business - "This is a must own!" For example, if you are targeting clients that want to lose weight, then try this - "For those of you that would like to get healthier than ever before, this book written by Dr. Christa is a must own." That would grab the attention of anyone that wants to live a healthier life, and it's a must own. Those two little words convey to the reader that they can't live without that product.

Word #7: Listen

When you say listen, everyone looks up. Try this – "Listen, pay very close attention to this." How does this sound? Don't your ears automatically perk up? That's how you grab your clients' attention and keep them on edge to see what you are going to say next.

Word #8: Best Price Ever Offered

"Tonight and tonight only, this is the best price that I've ever offered so you're definitely going to want to take action on this deal." Your customer knows that you've never done a deal like this before so they better grab a hold of it now.

Word #9: This Gets the Job Done

"For those of you that would like to overcome fear, the Lifestyle Freedom Club membership gets the job done. You will overcome the fear in your life now!"

Your buyer will fully understand that investing in your services will get the job done for them and there's no use in going anywhere else for what they want.

Word #10: Warning

"WARNING – do you have zero leads? Are you constantly frustrated about your lead flow? Then you'll want to own our lead generating CD teaching." Warning *(in all caps)* makes the reader aware that the information they are about to see is so huge that it needs a warning label. Every time I speak at a large event, I always put a WARNING Success Disclaimer in the very beginning of my presentation to WARN the attendees that the information that I'm going to teach them will change their lives forever. Warn your customers that your services will bring dramatic results in their lives like no other. They don't need to go anywhere else, because your services are the very best on the market.

Word #11: Probably the First to Sell Out

"This offer that you're about to hear about will probably be the first to sell out within twenty-four hours." That's awesome, isn't it? Remember, you're marketing to people who want to invest in your product before it's all gone, so let them know that it will be the first to sell out so they need to grab a hold of it now!

Word #12: Decision

"Now is decision time for you. Are you going let fear keep destroying you? Are you going let fear keep robbing your dream? It's time for you to make the decision to annihilate fear out of your life forever!" The word decision in Hebrew means to cut off. When your customers make a decision, they cut off the indecision that was stopping them from investing in your product. It's your responsibility to drive them to make the decision that they've procrastinated on for way too long and change their lives!

Word # 13: Proven, Time-Tested

How can you not believe someone when they tell you their product is proven and time-tested? This further demonstrates that you are a business person with great ethics that deeply cares for your customers. You want to give them only the best that you've taken the time to test and proven to be the very best. "This closing book is full of proven, time-tested techniques that will explode your business." There's no reason for the client to doubt whether or not the book will assist them since the information has already been tested and proven to work better than anything else on the market for real people just like them.

Word #14: Testimonial

Do you understand that 99% of your buying decisions in your life have been made on testimonials? As consumers, we want to know that someone else tried a product or service and had great results before we invest in it. Take a look at your business. Is at least 90% of your business testimonial based? It should be, because 90% of your own personal buying decisions are based upon testimonials from others. If you're not using the testimonials of your current customers to promote your products or services, then you are wasting millions of dollars per year. Start today by asking your clients what they like best about your products and services. Ask their permission to use the testimonials to promote your products and services to others. This will catapult your business and take it to a new level!

Word #15: Real People, Real Results

Real People, Real Results! Your clients and customers will be able to relate to and identify with this personally since they are real people and they want real results. Here's an example for you. "My motivational marketing products are used by real people with real results. Just take a look at these testimonials." There are so many fake stories out there used in marketing that it's refreshing to know that your company promotes real people with real results...REAL!

Word #16: Value

This is an essential word to use in your marketing. When I market my products, I always put a value on the CD or whatever I'm marketing at the time. It should be the legitimate value of your product or service.

After stating the value, clearly state the sale price or savings. This allows your customer to know exactly what they are getting for their money plus how much they are saving on the deal that you are offering.

Word #17: Bonus

"Today and today only, we have a very special bonus for you. It's a tremendous value, it's ridiculous, believe me. I warn you, this is shocking." Everyone loves a bonus! You can never give too many bonuses in your marketing. Bonuses not only excite the client to invest in your product, but they also provide a great incentive for the customer to buy your product right now without hesitation.

Word #18: Replace

"You can replace all of your so-called motivational products with our proven formula that really works!" Whatever you're trying to sell your clients, you can show them how easily your product can replace what they are currently using. "Replace all your real estate confusion with my expertise." You are basically showing your clients how easy the transition will be and how much more your products will benefit them.

Word #19: As a Matter of Fact

"As a matter of fact, my property management company was ranked number one in South Florida based on the testimonials of my clients." Your customers want solid facts! There's too much fiction in the world and too many people are wasting money on things that simply don't work. Provide your clients with solid facts that sell them on your products and services above others.

Word #20: Dissatisfied

"Are you currently dissatisfied with your marketing success? Are you currently dissatisfied with your chiropractor? Are you currently dissatisfied with your eye care?" There is dissatisfaction in every business so anyone can use this one! Michael Dell created a billion-dollar company going after dissatisfied clients. One of Dell's number one marketing campaigns was "Are you currently dissatisfied with your laptop?" He didn't go out and try to create the market. He wisely went after a currently dissatisfied market. You can do the very same thing in your business and marketplace!

Word # 21: Spoken For

"You must take action right now before these seven packages are spoken for." You're letting your buyers know that your offers are selling out fast so they need to take action before it's too late!

Word #22: Limited availability

"This event will change your life! However, there is limited availability based on first come, first serve basis." Limited availability instantly creates an atmosphere of urgency. No one wants to be left out or miss out on a great deal.

Word #23: Tonight & Tonight Only

"This sale is only available tonight and tonight only so take action now!" When you use this in your marketing, then whatever you're offering should only be available for that specified timeframe.

Word #24: We Don't Cut Corners

"We are Di Lemme Development Group, and we don't cut corners. We make sure you're fully satisfied with the product." Your clients don't have to worry about the old sale and bail routine from your company. They know that you will be there for them before and after the sale and look forward to building a long-term, profitable relationship with them.

Word #25: No Need to Say Anymore

"This deal will end tonight! No need to say anymore! Pick up the phone and grab a hold of this offer now!" You have put all your cards on the table about whatever you're marketing, and there's nothing more to be said. You are the best choice, have the best product and your customer need look no further!

Word #26: We're Not Just Another...

"We're not just another self- development company. I'm a strategic millionaire business coach focused on assisting you with the achievement of your Why in life." This will show your customers that you are not like every other company out there. You are different and will rise above all the rest, because of your proven results and your confidence.

Word #27: Amazing Breakthrough

"Amazing advertising and marketing breakthrough; amazing design company breakthrough; amazing real estate breakthrough." You're confident that your services will help your clients achieve the breakthrough that they so desperately need. You know it so all you need to do is let them know it too in your business marketing materials.

Word #28: Announcing...

Do you have a new product? A new monthly special? A new service that will benefit your clients? Announce it! "Announcing...the #1 secret to gaining more clients and making more money." Your clients won't know about it if you don't tell them so announce it to the them and the rest of the world! When announcing something new in your marketing, you need to make it exclusive and exciting to your customers.

Word #29: Your Shortcut to...

"Your shortcut to feeling healthy, your shortcut to great tasting food, your shortcut to overcoming fear." What is your business creating a shortcut to? Everyone loves a shortcut to the destination that they desire. It's your job to give it to them in your marketing.

Word #30: The Answer to Your (.....) Prayers

"My services are the answer to your financial prayers that will save your business." As long as your product and services are ethical and moral, you have a right to be the solution to anyone's problem and even answer a few prayers while you're at it.

Word #31: America's Foremost Expert

"I am America's foremost expert in providing quality childcare to your little ones." You're an expert in your business and can provide high-end services for your clients so be confident in your abilities. If you don't believe that you are the very best at what you do, then no one else will believe in you enough to do business with you.

Word #32: Your Partner in...

"I'm your partner in saving money on your mortgage that will help you find the home of your dreams." Everyone likes to know that they are not alone in finding a product or service especially when it's as significant as buying a home or car. You are there to provide your customers with the support that they need with their buying decisions.

Word #33: Straight Talk About...

"This is the straight talk about how to overcome fear in your life." It's simply straight talk about what you and your business can do for your customers. People will ultimately respect you being straight forward without all of the fluff.

Word #34: Create Fever

"We have created success fever for the members of the Lifestyle Freedom Club for over the past ten years." Whatever it is you do or specialize in, just put the word or words in front of fever to create excitement for your product. Fever is contagious.

Allow your customers to get the fever for your products and services!

Word #35: Break Away From the Pack

"How would you like to break away from the pack with my specific insider secrets on how to close on a piece of real estate and earn a huge commission?" Your business will allow your customers to break away from the pack and gain a competitive edge in their market.

Word #36: The Truth About...

"I'm going to share with you the truth about how to make your quarter million dollar home look like a four million dollar home with some extremely simple decorating tips." Revealing the truth in your marketing is not only an attention grabber, but a trust builder.

Word #37: *Quick and Easy*

Everyone wants business to be quick and easy in today's microwave society. So, quick and easy in your marketing will get people to pay attention. The whole idea is for someone to actually pay attention to what you're saying and then for them to call you back so you can make the sale. Example: "I will provide you with a *Quick and Easy* solution to your courier service nightmare. No more late packages, and I'll do all the work!"

Word #38: No More

"No more worries about fear. No more worries about unethical realtors. No more worries about eye care." What is it that your clients can stop worrying about thanks to you and your business?

Word #39: How to Discover the Truth About

"I'm going to show you how to discover the truth about financial services." Your clients are searching for the answers to their problems so it's up to you to show them how to discover what they've been searching for. No more wasting time or money on things that don't work. You've got the product or service that will lead to that discovery of truth and ultimately solve your customers' problems.

Word #40: End Your...

"End your wardrobe dilemmas with a personal fashion stylist." Once again, you're providing a solution to the customer's problem. The search is over.

Word # 41: How to Stop...

"Need to know how to stop leaky roofs? Call me." Your customers will instantly learn how to stop big or small problems with your products and services.

Word #42: Time Out

Time out is a subliminal subconscious word that makes you stop what you are doing. "TIME OUT everyone! Pay very close attention to this. Take a look at this amazing breakthrough. This will end all your worries." Time Out is telling your potential client to stop and take notice of what you're telling them about your products or services.

Word #43: *STOP*

The word stop grabs attention especially when used in all caps and with asterisks. I went to a $10,000 seminar on copy writing six years ago and learned that putting asterisks around action words like STOP will catapult your marketing results. That's why I use asterisks in every piece of copy that I write! The word stop should always be capitalized to emphasize that the reader needs to stop and pay attention to you.

Word # 44: Is This You?

"Is this you? Does fear keep you stuck? Are you wearing fear shoes? Well I can eliminate your fear through my proven, time-tested, strategic coaching." You've got to give your prospective client a visual that says, "Is this your problem? I can solve it." Address the problem head on and let them know you can solve it!

Word #45: I Warned You This Would Sell Out

"I warned you this would sell out and you still didn't take action. Luckily for you, I was able to get seven more spots opened. Now, don't delay again!" You're creating that urgency to buy before it's too late and they miss out again.

Word #46: Sold Out

These are two words you don't want said to you. No one likes to miss a bargain. Any type of business can use the words *Sold Out* when marketing its products and services to existing and new clients.

Word #47: Are You Kidding Me?

"You're still dealing with so-called business coaches that don't call you back. Are you kidding me? Why keep wasting your time when Di Lemme Development Group, Inc. is obviously the right company to meet your strategic business coaching needs and radically change your life forever." Your services are so good that it seems completely absurd that your customers would go anywhere else or continue to deal with those other companies.

Word #48: Frustrated

Everyone is frustrated about something! "Are you frustrated with managing your not-for-profit software? Are you frustrated with the customer service of your construction company? Are you frustrated with your legal service?" Get the picture of what I'm saying about this? You add whatever your industry is and simply ask if they are frustrated with it. You can end your customer's frustration!

Word #49: FREE

The word that everyone loves...FREE! Free is good. At my public events, I give the new attendees a free affirmation magnet, CD and newsletter plus other information about my company, products and services. Why? Because it's a qualified lead and I want them to know that I care enough about them not only to give them my information but also a few free bonuses. My elite coaching students have been trained to give out free one-sheeters to their clients that are packed full of information and advice pertaining to whatever industry they are in. Remember, free is good. Stop being cheap and start investing in yourself and your business by offering something FREE in your marketing materials.

Word #50: Danger

This is an attention grabbing word. Why? Because if something is dangerous, then people want to know about it. "My new exercise video is so effective in helping people maintain great health that it's dangerous to the prescription drug industry. I forewarn you...be very careful! Only watch this video if you are truly interested in achieving optimal fitness and health."

Word #51: Little Known Secret

You customers want to know inside secrets that can give them an edge when hiring a company to provide a product or service. Here's an example. "If your construction workers don't wear protective booties when they come in and out of your house, then they're going to make a horrible mess." That's a little known secret that most homeowners don't even think about when they hire someone to do home construction. It's a simple key fact that could save them lots of time, frustration and money in the long run. This is providing value to your clients that they will appreciate.

Word #52: You Won!

Winning is exciting for everyone! You grab the reader's attention and you give them something for free. For instance, "YOU WON a FREE in-home electrical safety assessment. Make sure your home is safe and secure for your family. To claim your prize, grab your phone and call (insert number) now!" Only use YOU WON if you are truly giving something to the person. No one likes to be suckered into thinking that they won something and then they really didn't.

Word #53: Conquer

This word can be used in showing that you are the very best in your industry and your services will dominate other companies. "XYZ Cleaning Company will conquer the competition by providing top-notch quality cleaning and superior customer service." You are instilling confidence in your product and service for your potential customer.

Word #54: Overcome

Using this word in your marketing will show your customer how your product or service will help them to overcome something in their life. "Finally overcome the stress and fatigue of holiday weight gain." Here's another example. "It's time for you to overcome the frustration of dealing with horrible realtors and not selling your home." You are basically freeing them of something in their life that they no longer want to deal with or simply don't know how to overcome.

Word #55: NOW

This one is easy. No one likes to wait for anything these days. Providing a product or service NOW is definitely something that people are looking for. Instant gratification! However, don't offer it if you can't do it.

Word #56: Solution

Make your product or service the solution to your customer's problem. A solution is a solid remedy not a quick fix so make sure that you are marketing it that way. "John Di Lemme's Strategic Millionaire Business Coaching is the solution to your failing business." You determine their issue and provide a solution with your products or services.

Word #57: Secret

This is different from the little known secret that we discussed previously. A secret is private and not known by anyone. It gives your customer inside knowledge about your product or service. Here's an example. "Grab your phone now and find out how you can instantly receive my*10* highly-guarded secrets about health and nutrition that most doctors don't want you to know." Remember, it's a secret so make your potential customers desperately want to know what it is and how it can benefit them.

Bonus Marketing Tip:

As a record-breaking, strategic business coach to Champions worldwide, do you know what really aggravates me? First time customer appreciation specials. It's like saying, "Despite the fact that you've spent thousands of dollars already with my company and you've been a loyal customer forever, I can't give you the discount because you're not a first time customer." So ridiculous! I'm going to say this again so listen up! First time customer appreciation specials are horrible. Why? Because you should give your past customers the very best deals. They are your loyal client base.

Conclusion

Turn your life and your business around right now! The information that you have in your hands right now will literally change your life and business. When you take these words, study them, and implement them in all of your business marketing material, you will achieve results like never before.

The only reason why you wouldn't implement these strategies and use them in your marketing is the opinion of one of your friends, family or co-workers that are infected with the fear flu. The naysayers will tell you not to do it and continue to do what everyone else does in marketing that simply doesn't work.

Do you really want to take advice from someone who is broke, going nowhere and miserable? It's time for you to think outside the box and get uncomfortable!

You are a Champion! You were born with the right to receive and achieve every bit of success that is coming your way. Vaccinate yourself against the fear flu, immerse yourself in personal self-development and apply the tools and secrets in this book. You are on your way to building a huge business and finally living true lifestyle freedom!

57 Must Use Words
Quick Reference List

#1: Shocking

#2: Absolutely

#3: Equally Crazy

#4: Tremendous Value, Ridiculous Offer

#5: Relationship Building

#6: Must Own

#7: Listen

#8: Best Price Ever Offered

#9: This Gets the Job Done

#10: Warning

#11: Probably the First to Sell Out

#12: Decision

#13: Proven, Time-Tested

#14: Testimonial

#15: Real People, Real Results

#16: Value

#17: Bonus

#18: Replace

#19: As a Matter of Fact

#20: Dissatisfied

#21: Spoken For

#22: Limited Availability

#23: Tonight and Tonight Only

#24: We Don’t Cut Corners

#25: No Need to Say Anymore

#26: We’re Not Just Another...

#27: Amazing (...) Breakthrough

#28: Announcing...

#29: Your Shortcut to...

#30: The Answer to Your (...) Prayers

#31: America's Foremost Expert

#32: Partner in...

#33: Straight Talk About...

#34: Create Fever

#35: Break Away from the Pack

#36: The Truth about...

#37: *Quick and Easy*

#38: No More

#39: How to Discover the Truth About...

#40: End Your...

#41: How to Stop...

#42: Time Out

#43: *STOP*

#44: Is This You?

#45: I Warned You This Would Sell Out

#46: Sold Out

#47: Are You Kidding Me?

#48: Frustrated

#49: FREE

#50: Danger

#51: Little Known Secret

#52: YOU WON!

#53: Conquer

#54: Overcome

#55: NOW

#56: Solution

#57: Secret